MARTIN LUTHER KING JR.

BY ANNE SCHRAFF

Development: Kent Publishing Services, Inc.

Design and Production: Signature Design Group, Inc.

Photo Credits: page 14, Flip Schukle/Black Star; page 50,
Black Star Photos; page 56, Library of Congress/National
Archives

ISBN-13: 978-1-59905-251-9

ISBN-10: 1-59905-251-2

eBook: 978-1-60291-612-8

Printed in Guangzhou, China

0411/04-81-11

15 14 13 12 11 4 5 6 7 8 9

TABLE of CONTENTS

CHAPTER 1

By the 1950s, African Americans who lived in the South were **segregated** in many ways. They had to ride in the back of buses and sit in the rear of theaters. Hotels and restaurants refused service.

African Americans of Montgomery, Alabama, **boycotted** their segregated bus system. A young minister, Rev. Martin Luther King Jr., led them.

King led a peaceful struggle for civil rights. He endured beatings and imprisonment. But he insisted on non-violence. King succeeded in making all of America a more **just** society.

Martin Luther King Jr. was born in Atlanta, Georgia, on January 15, 1929. His father, Martin Luther King Sr. was the assistant pastor of Ebenezer Baptist Church. A former **sharecropper**, King Sr. was a tough, strong man. The new baby was very healthy and was nicknamed M.L.

M.L.'s mother was Alberta Williams, a well educated and gentle woman. The Kings had three children. Willie Christina was older than M.L., and Alfred Daniel was younger. The family lived a happy life in a middle class, black neighborhood in Atlanta.

M.L. enjoyed playing baseball and flying kites with his friends. He rode his bicycle all around the neighborhood. Sometimes he went sliding down the banister of the family's two story house.

M.L.'s grandmother on his mother's side, Grandma Williams, was very close to M.L. She told the children stories and always supported them when they had problems.

When M.L. was a small boy, he was riding in the automobile with his father. Then, something happened that he never forgot. A white police officer pulled the car over for going through a stop sign.

The police officer came to the window. He called M.L.'s father "boy," even though he was a grown man. M.L.'s father told the officer to treat him with the respect he deserved. M.L. was very proud of his father for standing up to the white officer.

By the age of five, M.L. had a wonderful memory. He could recite long passages from the Bible. At six,

M.L. began singing in church groups. Everybody loved the little boy with the strong, emotional voice.

M.L.'s best friend during his early childhood was a white boy. The boy's father owned a nearby store.

The two boys played every day until the day it was time for them to start school. M.L. went to an all black school. His friend went to an all white school. But, M.L. hoped he and his friend could still play together after school.

Sadly, his friend told him their friendship was over because he was white and M.L. was African American. In the South, it was all right for very young children of different races to play together. But, when they reached school age, they were not supposed to be friends anymore.

M.L. began to notice segregation more as he grew older. Black people could not use the parks or eat inside a restaurant. When M.L. went to a shoe store, he was told to try on shoes in the back.

Sometimes M.L. was **disobedient**, and his father whipped him. When this happened, Grandma Williams would cry. This touched M.L.'s heart. He knew how much she loved him because she could not stand to see him punished.

When M.L. was twelve, his beloved grandmother died. He sobbed as if his heart would break. She was his best friend in the world. M.L.'s parents told him Grandma Williams was in heaven now. Someday, they would all see her again.

After Grandma died, the King family moved. M.L. was becoming a teenager. He was growing more rebellious. He continued to get whippings.

CHAPTER 2

As a teenager, Martin Luther King Jr. enjoyed wrestling, playing the piano, and listening to opera. Young Martin was a student at Booker T. Washington High School. He loved to read. Martin liked to eat too, especially fried chicken.

Martin loved his father. But he wanted to get away from him too. His father was a very strong person. Martin felt like he was standing in his shadow.

When Martin was in the 11th grade,

he entered a speech contest. He won a prize and was very proud. But on the bus ride home from Dublin to Atlanta, Georgia, something ugly happened.

Some white people got on the bus. The driver told Martin and the other black students to get up and give their seats to the newcomers. Martin was furious. But, he got up and stood in the aisle on the long trip home.

In 1944 fifteen year old Martin was accepted to Atlanta's Morehouse College. The college also got him a summer job on a Connecticut tobacco farm. Martin was thrilled to have his first real job. He was happy too that it was far from home.

The work was hard. He was picking tobacco in the hot sun. But Martin felt free because he was away from home. On the weekends, Martin went into

Hartford, Connecticut. There he saw movies and ate at diners.

Hartford was a northern city that was not segregated. Martin was delighted to be able to go wherever he wanted and sit where he pleased. He thought to himself that this is how it should be all over America.

When Martin started at Morehouse College, he did not know what he wanted to do in life. He did not want to follow in his father's footsteps and be a minister. He thought he might be a doctor or a lawyer.

While going to college, Martin lived at home. He joined the **glee club** and played football. But he soon found out that the college had very high standards.

He had gone all his life to all black elementary and high schools.

Unfortunately, he was not well educated. Throughout the South at the time, education at black schools was poorer. There were fewer books and lower standards. Martin had to study very hard to catch up, but he did.

After attending Morehouse College for a while, Martin was surprised to find out he liked his religion classes. He admired some of the ministers who taught him. At the age of 17, Martin decided that he would be a minister after all.

When Martin's father heard his son's decision, he was delighted. This is what he always hoped for. Martin's father asked his son if he would like to preach a sermon at the Ebenezer Baptist Church. Martin agreed and the people loved his sermon.

At the age of 18, Martin Luther King Jr. was appointed Assistant Pastor at Ebenezer Church. Crowds of people came every Sunday to hear the young man with the strong voice preach from the heart.

Martin was still in college. During the summer, he worked as a laborer on the railroad. At 19, in 1948, Martin graduated from Morehouse College. He then went to Crozer Theological Seminary in Pennsylvania to get his Divinity degree. Martin was one of six African American students at Crozer.

While attending Crozer, Martin Luther King Jr. began studying the philosophy of non violence. He read about Mohandas K. Gandhi of India. Gandhi used non violence to lead India to independence from Great Britain.

In June 1951 King received his degree. He was twenty-two-years old. After that, he was invited to attend Boston University in Massachusetts on a scholarship.

He fit in well in Boston. He found many friends and a special young woman who was destined to be his wife.

Martin Luther King Jr. met Corretta Scott while attending school in Boston. They later married.

CHAPTER 3

Coretta Scott was a student at the New England Conservatory of Music in Boston. She had a beautiful singing voice and dreams of a musical career. She was born on an Alabama farm. She had worked hard to get to the New England Conservatory.

A friend introduced Coretta Scott to Martin Luther King Jr. King fell in love with the lovely young woman right away. It took Scott a little longer to feel the same about King.

King told her that if they got married, she would have to forget about her musical career. He saw the role of a wife as homemaker and mother. It was hard for Scott to give up her dream, but she did.

In June 1953 Coretta Scott married Martin Luther King Jr. The wedding was at her father's home in Marion, Alabama. King's father performed the ceremony.

The newlyweds looked for a hotel for their wedding night. But no hotel in the area accepted black people. So they spent their wedding night at a friend's funeral parlor. Later, King loved to joke about this.

The Kings returned to Boston while Martin finished his studies at Boston University. At the same time, Coretta completed her work at the

Conservatory. Then, King looked for a job as a minister. Now Dr. Martin Luther King Jr. with a Ph.D., he was offered a job as a pastor. The job was at Dexter Avenue Baptist Church in Montgomery, Alabama.

Coretta King did not want to move back to Alabama. She remembered the segregation as she grew up there. She liked the North better. She did not want to raise children in the segregated South. But, she told her husband that if that was what he wanted, she would accept it.

The Kings moved into a shabby **parsonage** at Dexter Avenue Baptist Church in April 1954. King worked hard at his first **pastorate**. He visited the sick, prepared **sermons**, and attended meetings. The people loved him. He loved the work too. He felt he was really helping people.

In November 1955 Yolanda Denise, was born. Her nickname was Yoki. Both Coretta and Martin were overjoyed to be parents of a healthy little girl. But, **momentous** events were about to happen. These events would sweep the young minister into the spotlight.

On December 1, 1955, a weary African American **seamstress** named Rosa Parks was riding a Montgomery city bus home. She was asked to give up her seat to a white man who had just boarded the bus.

Black people were expected to immediately give up their seats if white people were standing. But, Parks did something unexpected and very courageous. She refused to get up. For that she was arrested and placed in jail.

The black people of Montgomery saw the arrest of Rosa Parks as a chance to do something about bus segregation. The United States Supreme Court had declared school segregation unconstitutional.

Now, they hoped to take the case of Rosa Parks all the way to the Supreme Court. They hoped that segregation on public transportation would be declared unconstitutional too. But, they needed someone strong and brave to lead them in this fight.

Martin Luther King Jr. was chosen as president of the Montgomery Improvement Association (MIA). This group planned to call attention to the unfairness of bus segregation. They were going to do this by boycotting the Montgomery buses.

Rosa Parks went to court on charges of refusing to obey a bus driver's order to yield her seat to a white man. The bus boycott was scheduled for this day. Thirty thousand black people, from children to the aged, usually rode the Montgomery buses. On December 5 they were told to all stay home or find some other way to get where they were going.

The weather was cold in Montgomery that day. King wondered if people would be willing to walk to school and work. Early in the morning, he waited nervously to see if the buses would be empty of black riders as he hoped.

CHAPTER 4

When Coretta and Martin Luther King Jr. saw the first bus coming down the street, they shouted with excitement. It was empty. All over Montgomery it was the same story. Black people carpooled or walked. The bus boycott was a huge success.

Rosa Parks was **convicted** and fined ten dollars. The conviction would be appealed. Maybe it would go all the way to the federal courts. Hopes were high that bus segregation could be ended and called unconstitutional. Meanwhile, the bus boycott would continue.

King and the other members of MIA made some demands as conditions to end the bus boycott. Black drivers had to be hired where the riders were mostly African American. Seating on the bus had to be first come, first served. If a black person had a seat, he or she could not be forced to give it up to someone who boarded the bus later.

Finally, many white bus drivers were treating their black passengers rudely. Elderly black women were called "girl," and mature black men were called "boy." This had to stop. Black riders wanted to be treated with the same courtesy as white people.

Many white people in Montgomery blamed King for the bus boycott. The bus company was losing money. White businesses in town were losing their many black customers. King received threatening phone calls.

Then, King was driving thirty miles per hour in a twenty-five miles per hour zone. The police stopped him. Instead of just giving him a ticket, the police threw him in jail with criminals. When many black people protested around the jail, King was freed until his trial date.

But the harassment continued. Everyday, hate mail came to the parsonage. Coretta King was worried about the safety of their baby. She dreaded the ringing of the phone because so many of the calls were threats.

King himself feared that something violent might happen. He told his followers that no matter what happened, they could not answer violence with violence. King looked at his wife and baby, and a terrible thought went through his mind. He realized that he might lose them if angry whites attacked the house.

King was so worried about his family that he felt he could not go on as president of the MIA. He prayed for strength. Then, he felt as if a voice were telling him he had to stand up for justice no matter what.

On January 30, 1956, the bus boycott was still on. King was at a church meeting when someone came to him with **dreadful** news. His house had been bombed. Coretta and his baby daughter were inside when it happened.

King rushed home to find his family unhurt. Only quick thinking saved them. Coretta King heard a thud on the front porch and ran to the back. The thud was a bundle of dynamite sticks. The dynamite exploded and ripped out the front window. Glass was sprayed all over.

News of the bombing spread through the black community. The people were angry. A large crowd gathered before King's damaged house.

Some of them talked about getting the people who did this. But King made a powerful sermon. He told them they had to love even the people who committed violence against them. Then, King led everybody in singing the old hymn "Amazing Grace." Violence had been **averted**.

The business people of Montgomery were losing a lot of money from the bus boycott. So, they demanded action. The county Grand Jury indicted Martin Luther King Jr. and the other MIA members. They were **indicted** for the crime of running an illegal boycott.

When King came to trial he was convicted. But King appealed. King's lawyers argued that the segregation of buses was illegal in the first place.

On June 4, 1956, the federal court agreed. When the case went to the Supreme Court, bus segregation was outlawed. The MIA won a great victory.

CHAPTER 5

In December 1956, Martin Luther King Jr. boarded a bus in Montgomery, Alabama. The white bus driver gave him a friendly welcome. King sat where he wanted.

Because of his success in ending bus segregation, King became famous all over the country. He was even known around the world. Newspapers from foreign countries wrote articles about him. He was the brave young black minister who stood up for his people.

On February 18, 1957, King appeared on the cover of *Time Magazine*. There was a big story about him. He was only twenty eight years old. Already, he had changed history.

Many black leaders came to Montgomery, Alabama to talk about the next step in advancing civil rights. Buses were desegregated but life was still far from equal for African Americans. In many places, they were discouraged from voting. Restaurants and hotels excluded them.

The Southern Christian Leadership Conference (SCLC) was founded. The goal was to use black churches to coordinate civil rights activities. King was chosen as president of the SCLC. The first thing on the agenda was the registration of new black voters.

In October 1957 Martin Luther King III was born. In the same year, King received the National Association for Colored People's highest award. The award is called the Spingarn Medal. He was honored for what he had done for African Americans.

But many white people were still angry with King for his work. They wanted the South to remain segregated. They were happy with the way things had been when black people stayed "in their place." That meant segregated and denied equal opportunities.

In 1958 King was walking to the Montgomery County courthouse with a friend. His friend had to deal with a legal matter there. King was going along to give him support.

As King and his friend reached the courthouse door, a police officer yelled at King to stop. They told King he had no business in the courthouse. When King tried to explain his position, he was placed under arrest.

King's arms were yanked behind his back. He was dragged down the sidewalk. Coretta King saw it happen. But when she tried to help her husband the police threatened her with arrest too.

King was taken to the police station. Then he was led down a long hall to a cell. Before he was shoved in, King was grabbed by the throat by one of the officers. Then he was violently thrown into the cell.

Martin Luther King Jr. was a famous man. But the officers who arrested him did not know him. They thought he was just an ordinary black man.

Black people were not supposed to talk back to white officers. When they told him to stay out of the courthouse he should have obeyed them. That was what they believed. But later on they found out whom they had arrested.

The Montgomery officials quickly released him. King told the world how he had been treated. He made the point that this was how most black men were treated in the South. This, he said, had to change.

Martin Luther King Jr. wrote a book titled *Stride Toward Freedom: The Montgomery Story.* In the book, he told the story of the bus boycott. He explained how bus segregation had been brought to an end.

In September 1958 King was signing autographs in a department store in

New York. A mentally ill black woman ran up to him. She stabbed him with a razor-sharp letter opener. The blade plunged deeply into King's chest. King was rushed to a hospital.

The surgeons who operated on him found the blade very close to the aorta. The aorta is the largest artery in the body. It was so close that any movement could have killed King.

The doctors worked on King for three hours. They removed a rib and his breastbone to get at the blade. Finally it was safely removed. King was saved.

In late 1959 Martin Luther King Jr. became co-pastor of Ebenezer Baptist Church in Atlanta with his father. Almost immediately, his enemies were at work.

He was indicted by the Montgomery Grand Jury back in Alabama for tax **fraud**. The people who hated him had bombed his house and had him arrested. Since that did not stop him, now they hoped to prove he was dishonest and destroy him in this way.

King never had much money. Most of what he earned he gave to the SCLC. His income as co pastor of his church was $6000 a year. He drove an old Pontiac and lived in a small rented house. He had no money to pay back taxes and penalties. He also knew he had done nothing wrong.

King's friends hired some good lawyers to defend him. They paid the lawyers because King could not.

On Monday, May 23, 1960, King stood trial. King looked at the twelve white jurors. He wondered how they could believe a black man. He thought surely he would be convicted. But the jury found him "not guilty." King was deeply touched.

With the tax problem out of the way, King turned his attention to a new cause. He wanted to desegregate eating places. For decades, black people could not sit in restaurants or at lunch counters. In the South, they could only be served on paper plates out the back doors.

In Atlanta, Georgia, King worked with a group of black college students. They were conducting a **sit-in** at Rich's Department Store lunch counter. King was arrested and taken to jail.

While King was there, the authorities discovered an old traffic violation of King's. They used that to transfer him to a tough prison for serious criminals. The prison was called Reidsville.

He was taken to Reidsville in the middle of the night in handcuffs and chains. He was thrown into a dirty, cockroach-**infested**, bitter-cold cell. King became ill and feverish. He was frightened.

Senator John F. Kennedy found out what had happened. He was running for president of the United States. He **intervened**, and King was immediately released. From then on, King and Kennedy were friends.

On January 30, 1961, Dexter Scott, the King's third child, was born.

In the spring, college students were going into the South to end pockets of segregation. They were called Freedom Riders. Martin Luther King Jr. took up their cause, even though he was threatened by angry white mobs.

The King's fourth child, Albertina, was born. King tried to spend more time with his family. He had been so busy that he worried he was **neglecting** them.

In April 1963 Dr. Martin Luther King Jr. joined civil rights demonstrations in

Birmingham, Alabama. This city was one of the most strictly segregated in the South. The police commissioner, Theophilus "Bull" Connor, was known for being tough.

King was arrested in one of the first protest marches. He was put in a small, dark cell. He had no mattress and no bedding. President John Kennedy learned what happened. He called the Birmingham authorities. Then, King received a mattress and a blanket. He was also allowed to shower and shave and talk to his wife on the phone.

King wanted to write down what he was feeling, but he had no paper. He wrote on scraps of toilet paper and in the margins of old newspapers.

The words he wrote became a famous essay that was published all over the world. It was called "Letter from a

Birmingham Jail." King said in the letter that black people were tired of waiting for their rights.

King was freed, and there were more large demonstrations. Children and adults were attacked by the police with high pressure hoses. Bull Connor's men beat the people with clubs and fists. All this violence was shown on television. The nation was shocked.

The authorities of Birmingham were very ashamed about what had happened. They agreed to desegregate the downtown stores. They also agreed to hire more African Americans and free all of the protesters who were still in jail. King had won another big victory in the civil rights **crusade**.

CHAPTER 7

Requests came from all over America for Martin Luther King Jr. to speak. He addressed thousands of people in Chicago, Los Angeles, and Detroit.

At the time, President John F. Kennedy was about to introduce major civil rights legislation. It would outlaw segregation on interstate transportation. It would also force school integration.

King believed this law would be of great benefit to black people. In fact, it would be beneficial to all Americans who wanted to live in a more just society. But a dramatic event was needed to bring the need for this law to America.

A. Philip Randolph came up with an idea. He was the founder of the largest black union in America, the Brotherhood of Sleeping Car Porters. He urged a massive march on Washington, D.C.

Black people and those whites who also wanted justice would take part in the march. King liked the idea. But many white people were afraid such a big march would lead to violence. Some people in the United States government thought Martin Luther King Jr. was a dangerous man. They felt he was a threat to America.

J. Edgar Hoover was the head of the Federal Bureau of Investigation (FBI) at the time. He feared that Communists, who were spreading revolution around the world, were behind King.

Communism was considered a real threat to the free world. In many countries, Communists undermined the government by stirring up minority groups. Hoover believed that was what King was doing. Hoover suspected that King was a Communist himself.

Hoover had a list of Americans he believed were enemies of the country. King was on this list. So, Hoover **planted** listening devices in King's offices.

He hoped to find proof of King working with Communists. He also planted listening devices in hotels were King stayed. He was sure he would be able to hear King and other Communists talking about overthrowing the American government.

Hoover feared that the march on Washington might be the beginning of Communist-**sponsored** unrest and violence in America. He thought it was going to lead to a revolution.

On August 28, 1963, about one hundred thousand African Americans and whites gathered. They were at the Lincoln Memorial in Washington, D.C. Another one hundred fifty thousand were on their way in trains, buses, cars, and planes.

In the end, over two hundred thousand African Americans and sixty thousand whites heard Martin Luther King Jr. speak. He delivered the most famous speech he ever made. It has become one of the most celebrated speeches in American history.

King spoke about a dream he had for America where all people, regardless of their color, creed, or background would enjoy equality. The speech was called the "I Have A Dream" address.

King's powerful voice and his emotional delivery left the crowd with wild joy. Many wept and others cheered. President Kennedy invited King and other civil rights leaders to the White House to celebrate. It seemed as if the speech had united everybody in America in the cause of justice for all.

J. Edgar Hoover was not happy. He watched King grow more popular. He still believed King was a Communist agent. Martin Luther King Jr. was a Christian minister with a strong faith in God. Communists do not believe in God, but this did not convince Hoover.

Hoover never found a link between King and the Communists. He did, however, find something that he hoped would destroy King's reputation.

After the successful march on Washington, King and his friends celebrated at a party at the Willard Hotel in Washington. The FBI had listening devices in the room. They picked up sounds of a very lively party.

Hoover sent copies of the tape to President Kennedy and other government agencies. He also sent a copy to Coretta King. Hoover believed the tape showed King partying with other women. But Coretta King **dismissed** the whole thing.

1963 had been a year of challenge and triumph for King. Before the year ended, it would be a year of tragedy.

On September 15, 1963, a monstrous act of violence erupted from the racial hatred in Birmingham, Alabama.

Birmingham's Sixteenth Street Baptist Church had been a starting place for many of the successful civil rights marches. On this Sunday morning, four little girls were getting ready to sing in the choir. Then, someone dynamited the church. The children all died. Martin Luther King Jr. admitted to being as near to despair as he had ever been.

On November 22 another terrible blow fell. King had grown very close to President John F. Kennedy. He saw the young president as a sincere ally in the cause of civil rights. Now, the news bulletin from Dallas, Texas, announced the assassination of President Kennedy. In his shock and grief, King told his wife that he felt sure the same fate would **befall** him, too.

President Lyndon Johnson succeeded Kennedy. Johnson pledged to make the civil rights bill into law.

In 1964 Martin Luther King Jr. was awarded the Nobel Peace Prize. King went to Oslo, Norway, to receive the prize. He pledged to give the entire cash amount to the cause of civil rights. He said in his Nobel address that the prize was not a personal triumph. Instead, he said, it was a recognition of all who struggled for justice.

In 1965 a civil rights march from Selma to Montgomery, Alabama, became a catastrophe. Hundreds of marchers were confronted by state troopers.

The troopers plunged into the crowd on horses. They beat and trampled the people. King was not in this march. But he led another march from Selma to Montgomery. The publicity helped President Johnson turn the 1965 Civil Rights Act into law.

At this time, the United States was fighting a war in South Vietnam. The U.S. wanted to stop the spread of Communism in Asia. Many Americans opposed the war.

Thousands of U.S. soldiers along with hundreds of thousands of Vietnamese had already died. Even though President Johnson firmly believed in the war,

Martin Luther King Jr. came out against it. He said it was a waste of precious lives. Also, the money would be better spent easing poverty in America.

King was criticized for opposing the war in Vietnam. Even some of his friends were upset with him. But, King continued to speak against the war. He also focused his attention on poverty in the northern United States.

Coretta Scott and Martin Luther King Jr. moved into a shabby old railroad car. The car was in a poverty stricken neighborhood of Chicago. It was on Chicago's run down west side.

In that area, there was no sign of trees or lawns. The house the Kings lived in had two bedrooms, a kitchen, and bathroom. The gas stove was broken and the ceiling and walls were crumbling.

Many Chicagoans lived like this. King said it was not right. Even poor people deserve decent places to live, he argued. The people who lived in these shacks paid high rent. King said they should refuse to pay another cent until the houses were made livable.

In December 1967 King planned a large demonstration to show his commitment to the poor of America. He wanted to bring thousands of poor people to the Washington monument.

He wanted a tent city to be built. The tent city would demonstrate that these people lacked suitable homes for themselves and their children.

King's plans to lead a poor people's march on Washington and his continued criticism of the war in Vietnam raised old **accusations** against him. The war in Vietnam was to stop Communism. King wanted to pull out. President Johnson was angry at King's comments. King's popularity sunk from its former high level.

But Martin Luther King Jr. continued with his plans. He was interrupted by another labor strike in Memphis, Tennessee.

Sanitation workers in Memphis called on Matin Luther King Jr. to help them get better wages and working conditions.

CHAPTER 9

Most of the sanitation workers in Memphis were black. They received low pay for dirty, dangerous work. There were no normal worker benefits.

Two workers were crushed to death in a garbage truck in February 1968. Their families were left with nothing. This tragedy called attention to the fact that the workers had no medical benefits. They had no unemployment compensation with survivor benefits either. The sanitation workers asked for better wages and conditions. But when they were turned down, they formed a union.

The sanitation workers of Memphis were on strike. But they were getting nowhere. The city planned to fire them all. In desperation, they called on Martin Luther King Jr. They wanted him to lend his **prestige** to their cause.

King's staff told him he had no time to get involved in the Memphis strike. King had promised to make many speeches all over the South for civil rights. There was no time to visit Memphis. But, in spite of this, King decided to go.

He told his staff that if he was fighting for poor people, how could he ignore these sanitation workers who had so little?

Martin Luther King Jr. planned to make a quick trip to Memphis. Then he would leave town and **resume** his speaking tour. He thought when he got there that he would be talking to a small crowd. But when he arrived at the hall there were fifteen thousand people waiting for him.

King made a powerful speech for the sanitation workers. He promised them that if the city had not yet met their just demands, he would come back in ten days. If he came back, he would lead a protest march on their behalf.

Memphis did not meet the demands of the union. So, on Thursday, March 28, King and other civil rights leaders led a march.

King had always insisted that all his marches be peaceful, but trouble quickly broke out. Young Memphis African Americans in the march started shouting. They committed **vandalism** along the march route.

The police charged in and the whole demonstration was a disaster. King was crushed by the turn of events. He planned another march. He insisted that this time it would be nonviolent.

On April 3 King returned to Memphis. He gave a strong speech asking for a nonviolent march. Those who heard him speak said they never heard him speak so **eloquently**.

The march was scheduled for April 5. King was sure it would be peaceful and effective. The sanitation workers would finally receive the justice they deserved.

Everything seemed to be falling into place. The local judge approved the march. King met with some young black men who promised to cooperate with him.

It was 6:00 on the evening of April 4. King and a fellow minister and civil rights activist, Rev. Ralph Abernathy, were getting ready. They were about to leave their room in the Lorraine Motel in Memphis. King went out onto the balcony. He began talking to some people gathered below.

There was a rooming house across the street from the motel. Inside one of the rooms was an ex-convict white man. His name was James Earl Ray.

Ray held in his hand a rifle. He was a drifter who hated black people. Ray's life was a bitter failure. He was filled with anger.

As King stood on the balcony, a rifle shot came from the direction of the rooming house. The bullet hit King in the lower right jaw. His jawbone was shattered. Then, the bullet drove into his neck. It tore major blood vessels. King's spinal cord was cut.

Martin Luther King Jr. lay on the floor of the balcony. Friends tried desperately to stop the blood pouring from his terrible wounds.

No one knew that King's powerful speech in Memphis would be his last.

CHAPTER 10

An ambulance rushed King to St. Joseph's Hospital. Paramedics worked on him until they reached the emergency room. There, doctors gave him oxygen and did all they could. It was not enough. He was beyond help.

Martin Luther King Jr. died at 7:05 p.m., April 4, 1968.

April 7 was named a national day of mourning. From all over the world came words of shock and sorrow.

Coretta King comforted her four young children with the religious faith that had been the center of the King home. Coretta King assured her children their father was in Heaven. She told them that they would see him again.

On April 5, Coretta King and her three oldest children marched in the sanitation workers demonstration as her husband promised he would. The city of Memphis immediately accepted all the demands of the union. The sanitation workers at last had justice.

King's body lay in Atlanta where thousands of people filed past the casket. The funeral was conducted at Ebenezer Baptist Church. There, famous people shared pews with King's many friends. King's body was placed in a farm cart. It was pulled by two mules to the cemetery where he was buried.

On King's tombstone were placed words from one of his greatest speeches: "Free at last, free at last, thank God Almighty I'm free at last."

Two months after King's death, James Earl Ray was arrested in London, England. His fingerprints were found on the murder weapon. At his trial he pled guilty to killing Martin Luther King Jr. Later, he denied it. He was convicted and sentenced to 99 years in prison. He died in prison in 1994.

After King's death, the 1968 Civil Rights Act passed. It made housing discrimination illegal. A year after King's death, his widow began to build a center. It was called the Martin Luther King Jr. Center for Nonviolent Social Change. It was located in Atlanta.

The Center's purpose was to spread King's ideals. In January 1982 it opened. The body of Martin Luther King Jr. was brought there. King's remains now rest at the Freedom Hall exhibit.

After King's death, cities, schools, and public buildings all over the United States were named for him. Martin Luther King Jr.'s birthday is now a federal holiday. Each year there are parades and public events honoring his **legacy**.

The true legacy of Martin Luther King Jr. lies in how he changed the social fabric of America. When his struggle began there was **rampant** segregation in the South. African Americans could not freely use public transportation or private and public facilities of any kind.

King led a nonviolent movement to erase the **blight** of racial segregation.

During his life, he insisted on giving credit to many people. He credited the hundreds and thousands of black and white civil rights workers who made his dream for equality come true.

But history will remember that the leadership of Martin Luther King Jr. was a powerful force. It made America a more just society for everyone. King lived for just thirty-nine years. But, because of him, millions enjoy a better, more just life, and a more promising future.

In 1986 President Ronald Regan declared January 18 as a national holiday honoring Martin Luther King Jr. His image appears on over 100 stamps in nations around the world.

BIBLIOGRAPHY

King , Martin Luther , Jr. *The Words of Martin Luther King, Jr.* New York: Pocket Books, 198).

Oates, Stephen B. *Let the Trumpet Sound: The Life of Martin Luther King, Jr.* New York: Harper and Row, 1982.

Witherspoon, William Roger. *Martin Luther King: To the Mountaintop.* New York: Doubleday, 1985.

GLOSSARY

accusation: a charge of wrongdoing

avert: to avoid

befall: to happen or occur

blight: something that causes destruction or ruin

boycott: to stop buying or using

convict: to find guilty

crusade: a strong movement for the defense of an idea

dismiss: to reject; to not take seriously

disobedient: not obeying or following rule

dreadful: terrible

eloquent: having the power of fluent and fluid speech

fraud: deception; trickery

glee club: a singing group; choir

indict: to charge with a crime

infest: to inhabit in numbers large enough to be harmful

intervene: to come between two disputing parties

just: fair

legacy: something handed down to later generations

momentous: very important

neglect: to ignore; to pay little attention to

parsonage: the home of a minister or member of the clergy

pastorate: the term of office of a pastor or minister

plant: to place in a particular location

prestige: reputation or influence due to success

rampant: spreading or existing everywhere

resume: to continue on with something

seamstress: a woman who sews for a living

segregate: to separate due to race or ethnicity

sermon: a religious speech

sharecropper: a farmer who gives some of his crops to the person who owns his land as payment for use of the land

sit-in: an organized passive protest

sponsor: a person or group that is responsible for something

vandalism: purposeful destruction of something

INDEX